Burying
Tom

Zenobia Harvey

Library of Congress Cataloging–In– Publication Data

Name: Harvey, Zenobia, author.
Title: Burying TOM / Zenobia Harvey

Identifiers:
LCCN 2020915754
ISBN 978-1-970135-58-9 (paperback)
ISBN 978-1-970135-59-6 (ebook)

Published in the United States by
Pen2Pad Ink Publishing.

Requests to publish work from this book or to contact the author should be sent to: zenobiaharvey@yahoo. com

Contents

Foreward

"If you always do what you've always done, you'll always be what you've always been."

Words to live by. I had the pleasure of meeting Zenobia Harvey four years ago. I have watched her growth, her deliverance, and her evolution. As the Executive Pastor of Ramp Church Texas, I have had many opportunities to work alongside her in ministry and as the host of the Women of Power Radio Show, we have worked together famously. I am so proud of what she has accomplished with "Burying Tom".

Tom represents the ever present things in our lives that prevent us from growing and becoming accomplished. This book creatively sweeps us into an undeniable journey from enslavement to freedom. The author's illustrations are so vivid and so spot on. It is relatable and revelatory.

This book is a must read for all!

Kasha Hunt
Pastor | Author | Radio Show Host

"Some of your most toxic relationships won't come in human form..."

~ Zenobia Harvey

Introduction

This book was written on April 29, 2019, just 4 days after "Tom" almost took the lives of others as well as mine. I was working on another book, but I couldn't finish. I am forced to believe that this book is why. It was a necessity for you and me.

Relationships. We want them. We need them. We crave them. They make our lives worth something. They can either be great ones or horrible ones. I've had my fair share of relationships, but there is one that tops them all. My 10-year relationship with "Tom".

You've always known him, but you did not know his name. You've seen him but I decided to keep him a secret because he publicly ruined my life and reputation. I won't blame everything on him. I take full responsibility for who he was to me.

If you've read this far, then that means that you have some extra time on your hands to read more. What I am about to share may not surprise some, but I guarantee it will leave others speechless. I just pray you can understand that when you've completed the story, it will help you make the decision to finally leave your "Tom". Ready? Let's go back to 2009...

Chapter One

How We Met

The year was 2009. I had two children, a job, my own place, etc. I lived a decent life. Nothing too bad. Just a normal 24-year old living life and working. No run-ins with the law. Stayed away from drugs. Paid my bills. Doing the mommy thing with some great help. I was raised in a pretty, tough area with an even more traumatic upbringing, but that was the past. I partied and hung out with my friends, but who didn't? I was at that age, I guess. I was just living MY BEST LIFE! (Yes! I just had to say that.)

I worked. (I heard that is how this "making money" thing worked.) I was a receptionist at a local doctor's office. I started when I was 18 because I had my son, so I wanted to make sure I provided as a mother. I would work Monday through Friday. Got a check and came back the following week to do it all over again.

I had hopes to go to college one day, but it wasn't a part of my "now plan" at that moment. So, I just kept working. I had some cool co-workers and patients I got close to. They taught me how to walk into adulthood. As the years passed the hours became extended, but the pay didn't match. There was over-time on our end, but no increase outside of a 40-hour check. You would think some of us would've left, but we didn't because we had our reasons. We were coming in early in the morning and leaving to go home to our families after the sun went down.

I will admit that I was not the perfect employee. I got in trouble like anyone else at any other job. At some point these hours began to wear on my body. My sleep was off, and I was always exhausted. At the time I knew of some sleep aids to help, but I never wanted to be so deep in a sleep that I didn't tend to my son.

Ambien was a no go for me; and I wasn't an over-the-counter sleep aid person. It's crazy because I hated medications and anything to do with them. When I was in high school, I drank too much cough syrup that was prescribed, and it caused me to literally pass out in class and... You know what? That story is for another day.

Back to my hatred of over-the-counter sleep aids. One day I went to my manager and asked her if she knew of anything that could help me sleep at night and she said absolutely. I just knew my life would get a tad bit better. That evening I was prescribed 30 pain pills of Lortab 10mg. My torrid love affair began with the love I needed to hate. Meet "TOM": An acronym for the "Torturer of Me".

Chapter Two

The Failed 180

"So, is this another pain pill story?" You ask as you roll your eyes.

"Yep. It surely is. Continue reading." As I return the eye roll.

I'm about to show you how "Tom" destroyed me and almost put me 6-feet under. I was in a relationship because the same way you loved, fought, cried, hurt, had fun in yours was the same way I was with "Tom."

The prescription was called in and I picked it up. I didn't think much of it because of where it came from. I mean, it wasn't like it was out of a trap house or something. Straight from the pharmacy. Nothing more.

I took it that night, and I'll be honest. It was the best sleep I had in a long time. I woke up the next morning, dropped my son off and went to work. I was feeling refreshed and started my day like any other day: Another day, one pill, and some great sleep.

This was starting off pretty good like any other relationship. My needs were being met and I didn't have to give much in return. As time went on, I began to like the feeling I was getting. As some of you know, pain pills were strictly for pain which is something I didn't have. I just had sleep issues.

By the way... if you take something that's intended for something else, be prepared for the unwanted results.

The feeling that came with taking these pills eventually went over to the next day. I was no longer taking them to get rest. I started to enjoy the high. It made me feel relaxed, calm, and more happiness than I've felt in years. Just like someone you fall for, huh? Making you feel all good inside. Well that was me. I enjoyed this feeling I got when I took these pills and I wanted more because that 30 ran out in less than 10 days. So, I got another one prescribed. I got that set, and it eventually became a normal routine. If I couldn't get it sent to the pharmacy, there were people willing to give me theirs. You'd be surprised what a great personality and looks will get you. I mean, I was getting 2 from this person, 5 from that one, and 3 from the other. Just to do some favors. Nothing crazy at that time. Just a little skip in the appointment line.

It didn't do any harm because they were all happy at the end. I started taking these pills daily and looking forward to that feeling. It was almost like my body telling me that I needed it. I would say I was taking at least 3 in one setting by the end of 2009. I started to get immune to it, so I added Somas. This is a muscle relaxer. Keep in mind... there was nothing physically wrong with me.

Taking these 2 together made me feel like I was flying. And I was getting it all for free. I became addicted to "Tom", but I didn't see it that way at the time. I saw how my focus began to shift from my children, my family, my home, my career, and everything else to this high I needed to have. My life was no longer my own.

I was in love with "Tom" and he showed many signs of a destructive character. I had no clue I would fall in its deadly path because to me, it was just pain pills and muscle relaxers. When you hear of people doing a 180, the hope is that it is for the better. Mine was for the worse of the worse.

<u>Chapter Three</u>

The Clingy Girlfriend

No one wants to walk into a relationship that will bring us down or kill us, but it happens. Some of us make it out. Some don't. In between, however, is where you figure out if you're the predator or the prey.

I was the predator in this relationship. The pills had done enough in the beginning to get me hooked. The prey did an incredible job because I never thought this would be an issue in my life.

This was what I wanted and what I chose to be with. More than any human being. More than my favorite food. CRAWFISH! Since I couldn't always get a prescription and people weren't always so generous to give me some, I began paying for them. At that time, they were extremely cheap, so it was ok. I could afford it because I still had a job. By 2010, I was taking 4 pain pills and 3 muscles relaxers in one setting.

Wherever you saw me, you saw "Tom", even if "Tom" wasn't visible to the human eye. My actions changed drastically. I would be holding a conversation, and out of nowhere, I would fall asleep. I would be smoking a cigarette and there would be holes in my clothing and on the couch from me nodding off. The feeling was so good that I would purposely not drink alcohol because I didn't want to mess up the moment of a great high.

I was dedicated to this relationship! My loyalty went a long way. Well, I take that back. Throughout this relationship, I did stray away and cheat with cocaine, mollies, and bath salts. Infidelity at its best, I guess.

At this point, close friends and family began to see a major change in me. I started to lose weight, got emotional all the time, forgot things that were important in my life, etc. Does this remind you of a toxic relationship? If not, it's because you're in one and you don't want to admit it or have never encountered one. It's ok, you'll know the signs by the end of the book.

Sadly, "Tom" told me exactly who he was from day one. I tried to change him into fulfilling something he was never created to do. Isn't this just like real life? I know. A person shows us who they are: a cheater, a liar, manipulative, jealous, etc. I mean I could go on for days. I can relate because there were times in my life where I wasn't always the victim.

I enjoyed what pills did for me. I never took the time to research the effects until it was too late. I was a like a thirsty girlfriend. *"Where are you?" "When are you coming back?" "Are you cheating on me?" "Can you take away this hurt?" "Can you save me?" "Please don't leave me!" "When can you make me feel good again!"*

I was desperate. There were times I refused to eat because wanting "Tom" was the only thing on my mind. I was so hungry many days and I only ate enough to make it to see the next. I felt like it was a form of cheating if I made my hunger my priority, so I didn't. My kids were being cared for by family on and off at this time, and bills were not being met. I didn't care. My selfishness for my high was my top priority. I never knew at this time how far I was gone behind this. It was obvious to everyone but me. They saw it. Some whispered. Some spoke up. Some walked away.

Chapter Four

Break Up to Make Up

As in any relationship, there were bad times. I was physically being affected by this. My body would go into cold sweats, I would shake real-bad, and my stomach would be in knots that created bad cramps. I could smell the sickness coming out of my pores.

When you feed your body toxic things, trust me, eventually you'll have an odor. The smell was like sweat mixed with medicine and puke. So, I would lay in the bed shaking like I had some type of disorder. The sheets would be soaked but I would stay under them because I was literally cold and hot at the same time.

"Tom" was taking a toll on me and like others, I tried to put my foot down and walk away. I remember this one morning I was so fed up with taking pills that I just quit. No nothing for the first couple of hours. I went in to work around 9 am. I could feel that something was wrong because my body started shutting down. I went to the back restroom, softly closed the door so no one would hear me, and fell to the floor. My body was curled around the toilet and my face was planted sideways on the cold floor. At that moment, that was the only thing that made me feel alive.

I almost fainted. I began crying uncontrollably. I could feel the tears from eyes my burning my skin. It was like everything started hurting. Soon after a nurse practitioner, who worked there at the time, came in to see what was going on.

"What's wrong, Z?" She asked.

"See...See..." I started slowly, "I... I've been taking these pills...and...and...I'm tryin' to stop taking them. So, I didn't take any today. Now...I... my...my body is...just..."

Her facial expression exploded. "Girl, what is wrong with you? You don't just quit like that. You can kill yourself!" This just hurt me even worse. I felt like there was no way I was going to walk out of this alive.

I knew this thing was killing me, but I made up mind that if I went back, I could take control of it. I could run this relationship. I could call the shots. I could change its effect on my life.

Sooo...how does this relate to a human relationship? We tell ourselves "I'm not goin' back to him!" or "I'm never gone date her again." But...somehow, we believe them when they say they have changed. In truth, the only thing that has probably changed is the increase in lies they have up their sleeves.

"Tom" promised me rest and peace and sleep. Naw, I'm lying. He told me exactly who he was and I just changed who I thought he should be. He didn't tell me about his other baggage. I just kept going downhill. Every time I would muster up the guts to leave, it called me to come back home. Reminded me of Pookie from New Jack City, "It keep callin' me!" Except that joka was saying, "Zowie!" Either through my relationships with others, my anxiety, or just my inability to know that I was good and strong enough to be alone. However, in 2010, I was done!

In September 2010, I started taking a pill to help me get off pain pills called Suboxone and I quit my job. This was the first time I felt free. I remember sitting in my car with my daughter's dad and the sky never seemed more beautiful than what it was at that moment. I felt alive again. I had finally been strong enough to walk away from what was trying to take me out.

I left the job and decided to move on. I thought quitting from the place where I started taking pills would be the answer. Nope. That only lasted for a split second.

When something wants you, it has a way of finding you even if you don't want to be found. Now I became the prey. Deep down I loved pills, I just hated what it turned me into, an addict. But I soon went back, and it got worse. We always broke up and got back together. I just tended to be the weak one because he had many other relationships with other people. Just like a... never mind.

Chapter Five

The Me I Never Knew

I was really, Really, REALLY bad off. I found myself defending pills like we defend those toxic folks in our lives. I would hide the fact and lie about being on them just like you would lie about being with that crazy, disrespectful, violent boyfriend or girlfriend of yours. I became a zombie in my own eyes, but I was fine with it.

I started losing friends and family. Lifelong friends. Family who had once been inspired by me. I could see the hurt in people's face. What they didn't know is that I drowned myself more in my addiction because of their disappointment in me and their abandonment of me. I remember asking my sister why she didn't stay around, and she said, "I didn't know how to deal with addiction. It was something I never had to do." I could see in her face that me being addicted truly hurt her. At the time I didn't understand, so I became extremely depressed. I can remember one time calling her while I sat in the garage cutting my wrist. I just cried and cut. I still have the marks to this day.

My hope was that someone would see me and care. Even if they yelled that I was crazy and stupid for cutting myself. Their response is all I needed. My friend tried her best to calm me down on the phone, but I just wished someone would kill me. I felt incapable of ever being back normal.

People always want to say, "Just quit" or "I did such and such...and it worked for me". Trust me, if it really were that simple, I would have quit sooner. I felt my kids should've had a better mother. My mom should've had a better daughter. Life really had no need for me. I didn't have a job, lost my home, had no car, and lived off other people. I was a deadbeat mom but a "Super Girlfriend" as an addict.

I had no job or no money to buy what I needed. I was up to 7 or 8 pain pills by this time with packs of cigarettes a day. What does an addict like me do next? Prostitution. I sold my body. I wasn't on the corner with my thumb out, but I was in somebody's bed or in some motel room.

I thought I was too good to donate plasma, but I was qualified to lay in someone's bed. (I still get a little upset that this was a walk I allowed myself to take in life. But hey, there's a reason for everything.) I got to a point to where I was making so much a night that by the next morning, I was broke. I spent it on pills, cigarettes, gambling, and random people I came across. I told some people about how much I made. Sadly, after I was done laying on my back, I would have the nerve to call it a blessing.

Whew chile, if I only knew better. I was making as low as $20 and up to $140, sometimes over $200. Depended on who it was I was with at the time. Sometimes, I didn't get any money, just pills. I remember one time letting this man use my SUV for like a month just so I could feed my habit. He was a drug dealer and eventually got locked up for attempted murder. Ain't no telling what he did in that SUV, but I didn't care. I was lying to get money. I was going as far as making up emergencies for my kids! The sad part is that I probably hardly ever spent a dollar on them with that money. And... I had the nerve to get mad if people didn't give it to me. Like, I would go off!

When I couldn't get my hands on anything, I would take the lower dosage like Tramadol or Xanax. I would go through a bottle of Nyquil, Advil PM, Benadryl, or whatever had drowsiness attached to it just to feel something. And if I saw children medication meant for sleep, it was gone that night. I would never allow myself to go sleep. I wanted to feel whatever effect the over the counter meds had. I was looking at myself from the inside, and I was headed to my grave.

I was locked up in 2011 while pregnant with my 3rd child and gave birth in 2012. CPS was called on me in the hospital because I had drugs in my system (pills). "Tom" was having his way with me and I didn't care about how my life was fading away with each that went by. Fortunately, my kids weren't taken. They ended up living with family members. I mean, it was bad. I was losing everything.

One day I was driving and blasting music while passing my family's home to show off. There was only parking on the other side of the street, so I had to make a U-turn. As soon as I started turning, my body went limp and the car stopped right dead in the middle of the street.

What no one knew is that I had popped so many pills just half an hour before because I wanted my high to increase. My family thought I was drunk but soon found out I was high. My brother carried me to the house, and I can remember my daughter crying. Not because she was scared, but because she knew what I did.

She was with me when I got the pills. That's when I believe my relationship with my family truly turned sour. It's a hard thing being the person that everyone thinks will succeed but only turns out to be a drug addict.

I used to think prescription pills were ok, you know. And over-the-counter meds were harmless. So, I thought. I was too bougie to put a pipe to my mouth and smoke crack or shoot a needle up my veins. I remember telling a close friend that at least I wasn't getting a prescription from the doctor, and I was paying for it by the pill.

He said *"You sound like a real addict. Why wouldn't you get the prescription if it were prescribed? But you'd rather pay $5 a pill?"* I believe that in my mind at that time, I thought if I accepted the prescription it was my way of saying I had a problem. I didn't realize that God had plans for me even then.

I just was happy to be alive and able to go get more pills. A lot of us come to a point where we are no longer who we were when first started these horrible relationships. Some folks didn't even recognize me. I had a broken tooth, weighed 110lbs, and my hair had developed a dread because I kept it in a bun and never washed it.

I think what hurt most is knowing I hurt my mom. She rarely said anything, but she was hurting watching her daughter die. I was no longer Zenobia. Yet, even still in this moment, seeing another person's hurt from my self-inflicted pain wasn't enough.

<u>Chapter Six</u>

The Fight to Get Out

We all have some type of fight in us. Some more than others. I had a fight in me to get out of this relationship. I was at the end of my rope. I burned relationships with many people I loved. I hated myself for how I treated my kids. I cried out to God to help me. That answer would come in a way that I would least expect it. After realizing that trying to cut my wrist and sleeping my days away wouldn't change anything, I slowly tried to fight my way out.

The fight started in 2015. I was beyond weak. To add insult to injury, my fourth child's father was murdered. I saw crime tape, police cars, and a bullet hole through the driver window. On the other side of that driver door was a man that I had known since I was 13. A man that I had been in relationship with on off for many years. A man who, at one point in my life, had every bit of my heart. This man I once loved was just killed by the police. I stood there and just waited for the scream to come out and the tears to fall. Instead, my life froze. Over and over, I could only replay what God had just told me: "Change your life or you're next." Now this wasn't to say that's why his life was taken, it was just God knowing this would be the only way to get my attention. It was my wake-up call. I slowly started pulling away from "Tom".

In 2015, I joined The Ramp Church of Texas (The best church EVER!), but I began playing around with the pills again. I was going to church high and leaving to get even more high and drunk. Yeah...God wasn't having it. AT. ALL!

One night in August 2016, I had a dream I overdosed, and I thought it was real because I had done it before. Wait. Let's rewind for a second.

A few years back, I saved a lot of bath salt or mollie particles that I scraped off the floor. Seriously...I literally dug my fingers in the carpet, pinching every piece that I could get. When I got all of it up, I shoved it down my throat.

Immediately, my heart started pounding. My throat tightened. My breathing slowed down. I ran to the restroom while everyone else was in the other room. I was scared to ask them for help because I knew they would go off on me for taking it. I never really told anyone about this in depth, but this was the one time I can say I saw myself dying because I overdosed.

I was so scared. I begged God to let me live. I stared at myself in that mirror. I wanted to reach out and save myself, but I couldn't. It was the one time I felt sorry for myself, and I was hopeless. I ran downstairs, drank some milk, and went back to the room and just prayed. I thought that would have stopped me, but it didn't.

Now back to this dream I had. I was in a restroom and I had taken a hand full of pills. I then slowly began to die. I saw myself in the mirror trying to speak but I couldn't move my mouth. I was trying to scream for help, but I couldn't. At that point I was like "I'll just ask God to save me again."

So, I called Him as my body was falling to the floor, but I didn't get the response I wanted. Out of nowhere, I saw this hand reach in and snatch me into the darkness and heard a voice say, "Not this time!" I jumped up out of my sleep and started crying. I was terrified! I swore that I would never touch any of it again.

After that, I started getting back on my feet. Got a job, started being a better mother, mended some friendships, and really got on the right path. Isn't that how it works? You get away from that bad relationship and life begins to go well for you. I truly thought I had ended this horrible relationship.

I was going to church, making inspirational videos, etc. I mean God truly saved me. There was a fight in me that I never knew existed. I struggled sometimes with being concerned with how people saw me now. I had done so much.

There are some people to this day that may never forgive me and will never forget what I did. I dealt with a lot of guilt and shame, but I pressed on. The one thing I cherished was that my kids never gave up on me. They never treated me different although they saw a lot of what went on. I'm grateful to this day for that and for them.

Sometimes our past has a way of reminding us of what we once did and the enjoyment that came out of the bad decisions. We can sit here and act like every bad decision felt bad or be honest and admit that there were plenty of times it felt good. The truth is that, even though I fought it out this time, "Tom" wasn't far from my memory.

I remembered how he made me feel. And some part of me wanted to feel the high again. I never understood how something so bad for me kept my attention. But this was about to be the fight that ended it all.

Chapter Seven

Ten Years Claimed Me, Eleven Would Never Make It

I'm sure as you can guess, "Tom" and I had an on and off relationship. I started back taking pills on and off, but it wasn't as bad this time around.

I was taking two at a time every other day, or I would skip weeks. It was random seasons. I knew to be cautious in how many I took and who I did it around. I started to sneak them and act as if I never took them again. I would lie and say my stomach was hurting or something to cover as a reason.

I'm sure people knew, and people talked. I just could not understand why I didn't quit for good. I started to think it would be this way for the rest of my life.

I used to cry afterwards because I was so mad at myself. I would call myself stupid and hated myself at moments because how dumb could I be to go back to what God delivered me from? How?

What I realized is that I wasn't really delivered. I was just operating in fear. Actually, it was the fear from the dream that pulled me away the first time. My real deliverance was about to come real soon.

I would always make an excuse for why I started back seeing "Tom". I would give a whole run down of my testimony and say it was my last time talking to him for real. This is the same thing that happens in other relationships.

We always make excuses for the one thing that is visibly detrimental to us. I believe it's because I knew that in my heart, I really wanted it to be over, but I just didn't know how or when it would happen. I even told people that when I called to not to give me any.

I went as far as deleting numbers, blocking incoming calls, and staying away from certain areas. Now mind you, this wasn't because I was back addicted. I did this because I truly wanted to stay away based on the damage it caused in my past. Kind of like when you were in a horrible relationship but towards the end there were those moments of going back but still trying to break free.

That's what I did with "Tom". One friend took me up on what I asked and said no. I was so angry. How dare he say no when I was paying?! But... his decision helped save me.

He read a text that I sent him months back in early January of 2019 which basically said how I didn't want to go back because I've come too far. How I no longer wanted him to give me any, no matter my excuse. How I really wanted to live right by God and do something with my life. As much as I hated him for rereading it, I thanked him because I had to eat my own words.

I never got any from him since. He would play around to test me and see what my response would be. Of course, I would say no, but that didn't stop me from occasionally going to the other spot across town with someone else. Every turn, I would take I was either being told no or no one had any.

There were times where I would thank God that I didn't find any because I really didn't want any. "Tom" had been in my life for so many years that at that point in my life I did it because it was something that I was immune to doing.

Now mind you, there was a battle going on within me.

A fight that wouldn't quit and that's because I knew God had a calling on my life and I couldn't give up. From 2017 - 2019 on and off I was still seeing "Tom". Only a few people I trusted knew because I knew they were praying for me. (See, it's necessary to keep people like this in your corner. People that see that there is a purpose for your life even when you don't.) I wanted out for good this time, but I didn't know how it would come. Well, in April of 2019 I got what I had been waiting for: My deliverance. It was the way it came, however, that shocked me.

It was my daughter's 13th birthday and I was trying to buy time until I had to get her. Some may frown at me but it's my truth and this time it was going to come one way or another. On that day I chose to take 2 pain pills and drink some alcohol. Maybe a can and a half with a shot of Whiskey. I hadn't eaten since the day before, but I figured it wasn't that much, so I was fine.

In all honesty, I thought I could handle it, I truly did. I felt a little buzzed but nothing that I thought would stop me from moving around like before. I got in my vehicle with my niece and my youngest daughter and began to drive. I began texting and driving, not focusing.

I decided to go an alternate way due to traffic. I had the music up, windows down, and I kept looking at my phone. I was in my Mercedes that I had just purchased back in March. I can remember my oldest son always saying, "Mama, don't be on the phone while you're driving." My response was always that I've never had a wreck. (That's the dumb statement some of us make to justify our illegal actions while driving.)

Now back to that day. As I crossed the light, I saw a truck in front of me on their brakes. It happened so fast. I saw the back of the truck, heard the hit, saw my hands go up, and heard the screams from the back. Then there was smoke from my car.

I was able to pull over in a parking lot and thank God that no one in either vehicle was hurt. The truck had no damage, but my car had a busted freon pipe and a damaged bumper. This was GOD! I say that because no one was hurt, and no police were called.

Pause: I have a strong sense that someone reading this is saying "I knew she was never off!" "She lied to me!". Wrong! I just didn't elaborate on all the details. And as far as being off, this was on and off. Not because I had to have it like before going through withdrawals, it was random. Only four people knew the truth including my oldest son.

It's not that they were the only people I trusted, but I knew they would hold me accountable and still encourage me to keep going. There was no way I would tell the same people that once crucified me because they would never understand that I was no longer addicted, but that I chose a moment to "relax" that cost me so much.

It may have not seemed like what I took caused it, because it wasn't enough to alter my thought process. But had I left early when I should have, I would have never put others in harm's way and never would've made those purchases. Had I not been texting, I would have never caused this.

At that moment I didn't care about the car. I tried to come up with an excuse in my head about why it happened, but the reality is that I couldn't run from the fact that I was careless, selfish, and lacked consideration for the life of my child and others. I kept visioning someone walking across the street and getting hit by me, driving on the freeway and hitting another car, or driving into oncoming traffic because of my stupidity. Texting didn't make it better at all because I had a bad habit of pulling my phone out.

What I didn't understand was that for years, I was far worse than this moment with what I consumed and never wrecked. I didn't even drink anymore but this one day I chose to have some. It'll always be the moments that you least expect, to make the most impact on your journey.

I cried for 3 days straight, but not out of guilt. I cried because I was hurt, tired, and exhausted. I remember my mentor saying, "Mistakes happen", but I cried back saying "No, it was because I was careless." Thursday, April 25, 2019 is the day my deliverance from "Tom" came.

It wasn't at an altar, in a prayer closet, or during Worship. It wasn't the taste that left or the feeling it gave me, but it was the fact that people's lives were at stake because I was irresponsible in how I handled taking it as well as being on my phone. That was enough for me.

I had traumatic things happen before, but this time I was overwhelmed with hurt and guilt. It came in a way that could only make me open my eyes to the truth of what's been holding me captive for 10 years. I realized on that day that I had been in a 10-year relationship with pills. That nothing, as much as I wanted, could come from it in a good way.

It had the same traits as a human relationship, just in a different way. I was tired and exhausted. I asked God to give me my old memories back. Those I had before I ever picked up anything. I just wanted to be reminded that I wasn't always like this. I remember speaking with a good friend a few days later and I just cried. I said, "When am I going to be free from this? Do I have to live the rest of my life this way?" He said something that pierced my heart but freed me. He said, "Your problem is that you're so focused on winning that you don't realize you've already won. Stop beating yourself up. Take it day by day. I'm proud of you, we're proud of you."

He was right. I went from packs of cigarettes a day, over 20-24 pills a day, cans of alcohol a day, selling my body every other day, and not having my kids to none of this being my now. I just was struggling with letting go. Deep down I had a fear of succeeding without it. I had gotten to where I could almost trust me, but not all the way.

It was time to walk away for good and that's exactly what I did. I quit! Eleven years would not claim me. I gave "Tom" his death certificate from his control over my life. No headstone. No obituary. No last words. No nothing but my removing his grip on me and my leaving him once and for all. I buried him in a place that he could never resurface. I left and never turned back.

Chapter Eight

Scared but Free

I slept for days after that. Went to work, came home, slept, and did it all over again. I believe it was my way of restructuring myself, my mind, etc. It was truly like how you get when you permanently leave a long-term relationship that did you more harm than good.

I sat and thought about every year, every cry, every person, every disappointment, and every moment. I knew I was I was different. I knew it was God. It wasn't that a pain pill was a sin nor the alcohol. I know people who take pills for the right reason and I also know occasional drinkers that know how to handle alcohol. It was that, for 10 years, I made them my priority. Anything that becomes your priority ultimately becomes your god, and anything that becomes your god outside of God himself becomes a sin. This is the explanation of "Thou shall have no other gods before Me..." These things could never continue in my life in any positive way because of what I made them to be.

I got up that Wednesday and decided to live. I had condemned myself enough. I got up and started cleaning my room, made dinner, and went to church before heading to work. I went to the altar and I finally cried the way a child cries to their parent when they feel hurt yet grateful.

I felt myself release all that I held to torment me. As I walked off, I embraced our Executive Pastor, Kasha Hunt. Sometimes you need to know people still got you even after you screw up. Worship started and I kept crying because I was grateful that God didn't give up on me. It's the worst feeling to think that God is disappointed in you, but I'm here to let you know that He is not. He is truly a loving Father. As I cried, I heard His voice whisper to me and say, "I am not disappointed in you. I just couldn't allow you to continue doing that and Me use you. The way I need to use you meant you couldn't bring that."

I told Him I was scared. I didn't know what life was without the pills. I didn't know if I could do it. I could feel the presence of peace, and He simply reminded me that I could do it. Then, there was a lesson led by an Elder in our church that summed it all up for me. It was the ending that started this new beginning.

She said, "You don't even know the value of deliverance until you know the value of yourself. We have intrinsic value." Honestly, I always knew that, but I fought it. I knew He had a calling on my life, so I knew this day would come. I just did not how it did.

I never thought it was fair that I had to give up everything to walk the road He chose for me, but He gave everything so that I could. We want to pick and choose what we want to hand over, but we expect Him to open both hands. It just doesn't work that way.

I'm here to tell you that life isn't over for you, and you are not the mistakes you fall to. The enemy attacks because he is threatened by your belief in God. He knows that if only a small percent of you believes who God says you are, he has lost. He uses things such as pills and alcohol to reel you in and take control of you.

But God has given you authority and power over him. Use it and don't you dare beat yourself up if you fall. Get up and keep fighting. I've been clean for over a year now. This is the longest I've been clean in 10 years.

See, the thing about leaving a relationship is that a lot of times it doesn't happen overnight.

It can be weeks, months, or even years. That's exactly how long it took me to leave "Tom". But you know what? I did and I'm free. Now it's your turn. What or who is your "Tom"?

It's time to break free. I'll leave you with this favorite quote of mine from my Pastor, Overseer Evan Risher, "Your only job is to trust Him. The results belong to God."

Special Thanks

I would like to give thanks and glory to God for being just that, God! He is a father that has always kept me even when I wanted to turn from Him. His love is something that can never be explained nor can it be fully comprehended. I'll forever serve Him and continuously stay committed to doing His will.

To my mom, Renea, the greatest woman to ever walk this earth. I love you with the depth of my heart that can never be uprooted. You're such a beautiful soul who took on the task of birthing & raising me and for that, I'm grateful. I'll forever run this race to make you proud. To the other mothers in my life: Regina Goldston, Kasha Hunt, Dr. Regina, Diane Moore, Sylvia Clardy, Roxanne Ford, Jacqueline Rockwell, and Erica Hill. I thank you all for everything you've done to ensure that I grew into a strong woman & mother. I love you all so much and thank God for placing you in my life at the time He did. It was necessary. To my brothers and sisters, definitely too many to name, but you know exactly who you are. I'm grateful for the years that had many ups and downs. We've been through so much, but we came out victorious. I appreciate you guys and love you more than words. This one is for you!

To my family and friends, thank you all for taking journey with me these past 35 years. God is so strategic in how He aligns people's paths and for that, I'm grateful.

To my Pastor, Overseer Evan D. Risher. Your yes mattered more than you know to this day. Thank you for leading me in truth, with love, through discipleship, and correction. I honor you in many ways and thank God for allowing you to be my Pastor. Thanks for believing in me.

To The Ramp, my family. Words can't express my gratitude for your encouragement, support, and love. You've been such a beautiful part of this journey and I'm grateful. I love you always... To my children: Jordan, Morgan, Coryan, and Kelsey. God favored me when He sent you guys. You have been the pillars in my life. You've seen my failures and my accomplishments. Yet through it all, you still love me no less. I hold the title mother because of you, otherwise there is no power in the word. My heart is grateful daily that I get to see you guys grow into beautiful young men and women of God. I owe you everything, and that's what I'm about to give you. You are my world and I'm proud of you all. I pray you're proud of me. I love you and this is for us!

Get connected with Author Zenobia Harvey on social media

@Zenobia Harvey

@zenobia_harvey